The Fantastic Adventures of

Oliver Phenomena

Oliver and the Little Bigfoot

By Andy Klein

This book belongs to

____

This book is dedicated to my family, who have put up with all my 'fantastic' adventures.

Look for other Oliver Phenomena books

Oliver and the Guardian Angel

Oliver and the Little Ghost

This is the big day that Oliver had been waiting for.

 He and his Daddy were going on a camping trip.

They had been planning it for weeks.

They were going up to the lake.

It was deep in the wilderness.

They would need to pack a lot of gear.

After a long drive to the forest, they found a

nice campground and began to make a

comfortable camp site.

Mr. P set up the tent while Oliver gathered

wood for the fire.

"Oliver, make sure you get a lot of wood.
We need it for cooking, warmth, and to
keep wild animals away."

"Okay Dad, I'll gather as much as I can."

As Oliver walked along he began to feel as if someone, or something, was watching him.

He turned to pick up a twig and saw a young bigfoot who was carrying some sticks.

"Oh, hello," he said. "Are you helping me to gather wood for the campfire?" The little bigfoot grinned and nodded his furry head.

"We have to get as much as we can," Said Oliver.

Oliver and Squatch worked together to bring lots of wood to the campsite.

Mr. P stared at the giant pile of branches in amazement.

He scratched his head and wondered.

How did that little boy gather so much wood so fast?

Sometimes, he just bewilders me!

After a day of setting up camp and collecting wood, Oliver sure was hungry.

Mr. P had made a nice fire and they were enjoying cooking their hotdogs on a stick.

Oliver loved the outdoors.

He thought being in the forest with his dad was just about the greatest thing ever!

He wondered if Squatch liked hotdogs too?

The next day Oliver was thrilled to be going fishing.

His dad showed him how to put a worm on the hook, and to cast the line into the water.

Mr. P only caught one small fish, while Oliver, with the help of Squatch, had better luck.

Squatch was an expert at fishing and quickly filled the basket.

Mr. P was a bit surprised, and somewhat dispirited.

Later that day, Mr. P and Oliver decided to go on a canoe ride.

They paddled out into the water and were enjoying themselves.

Mr. P was looking for birds and other animals. He did not see that they were headed for a big waterfall!

By the time he noticed, they were in trouble.

Oliver was frightened. He did not want to go over the falls.

As they were about to go over, Squatch reached down from a tree and stopped them from falling!

That night, Oliver and his dad sat by the fireside roasting marshmallows.

They were thinking about what adventures they had shared on their camping trip.

Squatch was curious as to what they were eating.

Oliver snuck him a roasted marshmallow.

Squatch didn't quite know how to eat it.

Oh! What a mess he made!

Oliver washed with cold river water. He brushed his teeth and climbed into his sleeping bag.

"This sure was a great camping trip, son," said Mr. P.

"It sure was Dad, I had a fantastic time," replied Oliver.

They rolled over and said, 'good night'.

Squatch let out a low snarl, and Mr. P looked leery.

He thought for a moment, and then went to sleep. Oliver smiled, and feeling his furry friend beside him, fell asleep blissfully.

In the morning, Oliver helped his dad pack up the car.

Oliver was sad to be leaving the forest, and his new friend.

"Don't worry Oliver, we can come back again," said Mr. P.

Oliver made sure the fire was out and jumped in the car.

As they drove away he saw Squatch and waved.

He was smiling as the little bigfoot waved back.